FOOTBALL
LEGENDS

# KYLIAN MBAPPE

## ED HAWKINS

# FOOTBALL LEGENDS
# KYLIAN MBAPPE

**SCHOLASTIC**

Published in the UK by Scholastic, 2021
Euston House, 24 Eversholt Street, London, NW1 1DB
Scholastic Ireland, 89E Lagan Road, Dublin Industrial Estate,
Glasnevin, Dublin, D11 HP5F

Text © Ed Hawkins, 2021
Cover illustration © Stanley Chow, 2021

ISBN 978 07023 0400 2

A CIP catalogue record for this book is available from the British Library.

Printed and bound by CPI Group (UK) Ltd, Croydon, CR0 4YY
Paper made from wood grown in sustainable forests
and other controlled sources.

5 7 9 10 8 6 4

While this book is based on real characters and actual historical events,
some situations and people are fictional, created by the author.

UNAUTHORIZED: this book is not sponsored,
approved or endorsed by any person who appears in this book.

www.scholastic.co.uk

# Contents

# THE BOY FROM BONDY

In Bondy, a northern and poor suburb of Paris, France, there are three murals which help to guide and inspire people through everyday life. They are of Kylian Mbappé, one of their own. The boy from Bondy who played on their streets and became the greatest footballer in the world.

The first is a picture of a young Kylian fast asleep in the green strip of local club AS Bondy, dreaming about wearing France's number 10 shirt. The second shows him wearing the kit of Paris Saint-Germain. "Bondy Ville des Possibles" ("Bondy, City of Possibilities") is the slogan.

Finally, the third has Kylian smiling in front of a French flag. It reads, "'98 was a great year for French football. Kylian was born."

In 1998, of course, France won their first World Cup. Kylian would be the nineteen-year-old superstar who would propel them to their second title.

Kylian is not just the face of Bondy – or that of Paris Saint-Germain, the European superclub who are aiming to take down giants like Real Madrid and Barcelona for Champions League domination – but of French football. It's not Paul Pogba. Or Antoine Griezmann. Kylian is more famous than the two of them combined.

He is known the world over for his blistering pace and brilliant finishing. For the records that he smashes. And for the list of trophies and titles that most footballers could only dream of. But Kylian is not finished yet.

He has a plan to win everything, everywhere. A plan which he decided upon at a very young age.

It is why when he was standing in the tunnel before France's World Cup final victory over Croatia in Moscow in 2018 that he felt perfectly relaxed and ready to enjoy the biggest game of his life. It is why it felt like he was having a kickabout with friends when he destroyed Argentina and Lionel Messi in the knockout stages.

Kylian was born for these moments.

This is a story about how he made them.

# READY FOR STARDOM

Kylian Mbappé Lottin was born on 20 December 1998. The apartment he lived in with his mum and dad overlooked the football stadium of the local team, AS Bondy. His father, Wilfried, was a football coach there, his mother, Fayza, was a former professional handball player and his adopted brother, Jirès, was in the youth team. Oh, and there was also cheeky younger brother Ethan, whom Kylian would play *FIFA* with all day if he had the chance!

It seemed inevitable to Wilfried and Fayza that Kylian would be interested in the beautiful game, but even they were surprised by the single-minded determination and obsession he showed from an early age. As soon as Kylian could talk, he was not shy in telling anyone who would listen (and those who wouldn't) that he was going to be one of the best players in the world.

Wilfried even has a recording of Kylian, at about the age of four or five, telling his dad exactly what he would achieve in the game. When he was six years old he would practise being interviewed by football reporters after a match-winning performance. He would answer the questions about the brilliant goals he had scored or the amazing solo runs to set up others. So Kylian's talent extended beyond football to predicting the future.

Cristiano Ronaldo, the Real Madrid star, was his hero. Kylian's bedroom wall was covered with posters of the Portuguese player. When he was playing football he would try to mimic Cristiano and told his friends he was going to be just like him. He also had posters of Zinedine Zidane, the legendary French World Cup-winning captain on his bedroom wall and, amazingly, Neymar, the Brazilian superstar who would one day become his Paris Saint-Germain teammate. Today,

Neymar finds this funny and refuses to believe it is a true story.

And if he wasn't playing football, Kylian was watching football. His dad remembers him sitting in front of the television for hour after hour. Sometimes he would watch four matches in a row if possible.

The only time Kylian didn't seem to have his mind solely on football was when his mum and dad bought him a toy 4x4 truck at the age of three. He was able to sit in the truck and pedal it around, pretending it was the real thing. They let him pedal down the street and across the road to football training. He was obsessed with it. But little did his parents know that Kylian was just imagining that he was a footballer driving an expensive car to training. Now he jokes "all that was missing was my bag of toiletries". Of course, when he got to training he didn't give the truck a second glance. All he wanted was the football, to run, dribble and shoot for goal.

## The Dreamer

Despite thinking about football all the time, Kylian still had to go to school. So what sort of student was he?

He was a daydreamer, often being told off by his teachers for not concentrating. Instead he was thinking about scoring goals or fancy tricks. He didn't like to be sat in a stuffy classroom. Kylian had too much energy! He wanted to be on the move, running, playing and kicking a ball.

His mum and dad thought – and his teachers now agree – that because Kylian was so convinced that he was going to be a professional footballer he reckoned school was just not for him. At the age of five, his mum was so worried about his schoolwork that she sent her son to a psychologist to check if he had difficulty learning. There was no problem. Kylian was very clever. Perhaps too clever sometimes.

When he was set an intelligence test at school, he passed with flying colours with one of the highest marks in the class. The problem was there was a second part to the test and when Kylian was told he had to take the exam instead of playing outside, he messed it up on purpose.

Kylian was cheeky, his teachers remember. When he was six, after he was told off in class, one teacher punished Kylian by telling him to "go into the playground and pick up ten pieces of rubbish". Kylian went outside, tore up a sheet of paper into ten pieces and came straight back. His teacher saw him do it. "Find me ten more."

At the age of ten, Kylian was sent to a Catholic school because his parents were still worried that he was not doing well enough at school. He had a report card which was given to children who misbehaved. At the end of each lesson the teacher would write down whether he had been bad or good. There were not very many good remarks. The teachers complained that he would answer back to them or tease them.

It was unusual for Kylian to tease his classmates, though. The one time he did do that, making fun of a boy for wearing a jumper, his mother taught him a lesson. The next day, she made him wear silly clothes – flared trousers and trainers with Velcro straps. His mum was teaching him to respect others.

Despite his parents' confidence in his ability they

told him it was important to have a good education in case football didn't work out. Kylian also had tennis lessons, sang in a choir and learned to play the flute.

There is little doubt that Kylian could not have made it as one of the top players in the world without a calm upbringing by his mum and dad. Fayza was desperate to make sure that her son grew up to be hard-working and grateful, not spoilt or arrogant. When Kylian was playing for Monaco she found out that somebody else was cleaning his football boots. She was furious. "I forbid you from having someone else clean your boots," she told him. "You come from Bondy with strong human values. Don't start getting into habits like that."

## 'Beep Beep'

Fayza and Wilfried met in the late 1980s at a youth club in Bondy. Wilfried then set up a new youth club, called Le Petit Bar. This was the start of a football revolution in Bondy which would produce many professional players. Wilfried would organise Saturday kickabouts, and soon they had so many kids wanting to play that they started their own league.

It was so successful that AS Bondy, the local club, realised they needed to be involved. They asked Wilfried to come and coach their youth teams. And soon the kids followed. AS Bondy now has almost 1,000 members and multiple kids' teams, including three girls' teams.

Wilfried, Kylian's dad, was a serious man who spoke with a deep voice. Everyone who met him respected him. Without Wilfried, there probably wouldn't have been the huge interest in playing football in Bondy. He had a huge influence on a number of players and Kylian was not the only one he helped to achieve stardom.

From the age of two, Kylian would go to watch and listen to his dad coach. He would kick a ball in the club's corridors and sit in on team meetings. He was so good as a young player for Bondy that he would play in the age groups two years ahead. He was nicknamed 'Beep Beep' after the character Road Runner from the *Looney Tunes* cartoons because he was so fast.

## Coach of Stars

Wilfried, Kylian's dad, has not been just a huge influence on his son's career. He has helped launch the professional career of other players thanks to his coaching at AS Bondy.

For a start, there are two France internationals. Jonathan Ikoné, who plays for Lille, and Sébastien Corchia, who has played in Spain for Sevilla and Espanyol, were both coached by Wilfried at Bondy. Other players he coached at the club include …

**William Saliba:** signed for Arsenal for £27 million in 2019
**Joé Kobo:** midfielder who played for Lille's B team
**Metehan Güçlü:** young striker who has played for Paris Saint-Germain and Rennes

**Fabrice N'Sakala:** left-back who has starred for Troyes, Anderlecht and Alanyaspor

**Mourad Satli:** defender who has played in Belgium, Romania and Qatar

**Steeven Joseph-Monrose:** winger who has had a successful career in France and Belgium

**Ben Sangaré:** attacking midfielder who has played in France's second league, Ligue 2

One of the most important footballing lessons Kylian received was from his mum. He was eleven years old and was playing in the semi-final of a local tournament. He described this match as a turning point in his life.

It was played in a real football stadium in Gagny, in the eastern suburb of Paris. Kylian had never played in a proper stadium before, nor had he ever seen so many spectators. It was the first, and only, time in his life that confidence seemed to drain out of him. He could barely kick the ball, let alone run.

Kylian can even remember the day of the week the match was played. It was a Wednesday. He says, "I was terrified. I mean, really, I practically didn't run I was so scared. I barely touched the ball. And I will never forget, after the match, my mother walked out onto the pitch and grabbed me by the ears."

She told him, "You are going to remember this all your life. You always have to believe in yourself, even if you fail. You can miss sixty goals. No one cares. But the fact that you refuse to play because you're scared, it can haunt you all your life."

Those words changed Kylian to the point that he was never scared on a football pitch again. It is why, when he had a trial at Chelsea soon after that experience, he was excited. It was why he was excited standing in the tunnel before the World Cup final in Russia. Before the biggest game of life. He was excited before his first ever professional game for Monaco at the age of sixteen. He knew he was ready and able to show everybody how good he was. No fear.

# ACADEMY STAR

In September 2011, at the age of twelve, Kylian swapped the hustle and bustle of city life for the peace and quiet of the forest. He swapped the comfort of home life with his family for a small room with boys he didn't know. He swapped Bondy for Clairefontaine, the world-famous French football academy which has produced some of the country's greatest stars.

Kylian was still getting into trouble at his school and his parents felt that he would be better suited to an education which was tailored around football. The family knew Clairefontaine well – his brother Jirès had attended.

For most boys it wasn't an easy decision to go to such a brilliant academy. In fact, it was not a decision at all. You had to be selected. Clairefontaine takes only twenty-three new boys every year. They pick the best of the best from in and around Paris. Thierry Henry, Nicolas Anelka, Louis Saha and William Gallas are all former students.

It is such an elite academy that a player has to be exceptional to be selected. Would you believe that Anthony Martial, the Manchester United star, and N'Golo Kanté, Premier League title winner and World Cup winner, were not deemed good enough?

Once there the boys are left in no doubt about how lucky they are. It is the first step on the ladder to becoming not just a professional footballer, but one of the best in France. Even the French national team train there for matches. It is state of the art, with five-star hotels, libraries, cinemas, seven grass pitches, three synthetic pitches, fitness centres and restaurants.

In the hallways there are pictures of all the famous graduates. One of them is Kylian. His face seems to be on every wall. He wrote on one picture, "Thank you for two wonderful years." There is even a special area dedicated to all the newspaper reports and headlines about Kylian.

Coaches and teachers work so hard to improve the boys' footballing ability. They focus on their technique, improving decision-making and timing how quickly they can turn with a ball and without. They take intelligence tests and are set puzzles to solve. Clairefontaine was the first academy in the world to be so detailed and obsessive about training young players.

Although it is difficult to be selected, there was never any doubt that Kylian would be able to go. As soon as the coaches at Clairefontaine saw him play, they desperately wanted him. They recognised that he was freakishly good for his age.

Instead, it was down to Kylian to select Clairefontaine. After the success of Clairefontaine, many clubs in France had copied the programme and set up their own academies, and Kylian had been very close to joining the French Ligue 1 team RC Lens as part of their youth programme that had developed players like Raphaël Varane and Serge Aurier.

So what happened? Just before Kylian was going to join them, Lens were relegated from the top division.

So Kylian decided it wasn't as good, and chose Clairefontaine.

## Slow Start

Thierry Henry is the player that Kylian has been most compared to throughout his career because of their similar style of play. But at Clairefontaine they were compared for a different reason: they didn't impress the coaches immediately. Thierry struggled to fit in with the players and was criticised for not working hard enough. Kylian's problem was that he could sulk if things did not go his way. So much so that he had a nickname – Mbebe (pronounced M-baby).

Why was Kylian so frustrated? Well, it was because he was so desperate to do well and be the best player. But he wasn't the best player and that used to make him angry. That was Arnaud Nordin, a striker who would score loads of goals, often supplied by Kylian who was on the wing. Arnaud now plays in the top French division, Ligue 1, for Saint-Étienne.

Still, Arnaud and Kylian were friends. Arnaud

knew that Kylian was being fiercely competitive and wanted to win and be the best at everything. Arnaud also said that Kylian was great fun and if they were playing in a match and he dribbled past him he would turn round and say, "Did you see how I did that?"

## Life at Clairefontaine

- Players attend from Sunday to Friday
- They play for their local clubs on Saturday
- All Clairefontaine teams train in the 4-3-3 formation
- Lessons start at 8 am and finish at 3 pm
- They train for two hours from 4.30 pm
- There is homework in the evenings. But if it's a Champions League night first-year students can watch the first half and second-year students the whole match
- If a boy is late for training he is made to run for the number of minutes he is late by. Ten minutes late, ten minutes running.

Away from the pitch, Kylian was really popular. He would play football in the corridors or *FIFA* on his computer with his first-year room-mate Armand Laurienté, who now plays as a striker for FC Lorient. Armand would be Barcelona and Kylian would be Real Madrid so he could be his idol, Cristiano Ronaldo.

At Clairefontaine, Kylian learned to be patient with his body. He wasn't the best because he wasn't as strong as some of the other players, like Arnaud, who had developed faster physically. He adapted his game. The head coach at Clairefontaine, Jean-Claude Lafargue, said that he stayed clear of defenders and made sure his first touch of the ball was made with extra movement to take them by surprise.

From Sunday to Friday, Kylian worked hard at Clairefontaine. He even played football when he was supposed to be asleep. When all the lights were out, Kylian would sneak out of bed, put on his training shoes and go outside with a ball, shining a torch to find his way. He would practise all his skills and try to recreate the latest wonder goal by Cristiano Ronaldo, all the time 'commentating' to himself about what he was doing. And once the ball hit the net, he would practise his goal celebration too!

On a Saturday he would play again for Bondy, coached by his father. And his dad made sure he kept his feet on the ground. Kylian remembers one game he was playing for Bondy when he heard the voice of his Clairefontaine coach in his head: "Work on your weaker foot!" So when Kylian received the ball on the wing, he worked the ball to his left foot. He tried a long pass with his left and lost the ball. The other team counter-attacked and almost scored. His dad was really angry.

"Kylian! You are not here to try your fancy Clairefontaine experiences! We have a league to play here! You can go back to Clairefontaine all week and train on your nice field! But this is Bondy! Here, we also have a life!"

That was an important lesson for Kylian. He was a player in a team. And for that team, winning was everything.

By his second year at Clairefontaine, Kylian had grown bigger and stronger. He would count all the goals and assists he made in training. The coaches said his game had 'exploded' in his last six months.

He could play with his back to goal, use both his left and right foot, was much better at tracking back, made clever runs off the ball and was faster than ever before. Also his finishing was excellent.

Everyone could see how good he was going to be. One coach said he thought he'd be a future winner of the Ballon d'Or, the yearly award given to the best player in the world.

# THE REAL DEAL

For his tenth birthday, a family friend of the Mbappés gave Kylian a model of the Santiago Bernabéu Stadium, the home ground of Real Madrid. They joked that one day they would buy tickets for a match. Kylian was not fazed. He responded by saying that he would get them seats in the directors' box – because he would be playing for the famous Spanish club.

Four years later, Kylian's confidence proved right. Real Madrid wanted him to go for a trial. Scouts had been watching Kylian at Bondy and they were wowed by his brilliant play. They had also been closely following his work at Clairefontaine. Kylian could hardly believe it. Cristiano Ronaldo, his hero, played for Real.

Real were desperate for Kylian to sign for them and they worked hard to impress the youngster and his family. For a start, Zinedine Zidane, another of Kylian's idols, showed him round the training complex. It was difficult for Kylian to take it all in and he had to pinch himself to check it was really happening.

It was the week of Kylian's fourteenth birthday, and this meant the Mbappés regarded it as a holiday and a treat for their son. Wilfried, Fayza and Kylian's brother Ethan all travelled too. His dad said: "We did not go to Madrid to learn more about our son's potential but to please him."

Would you believe that Zidane also picked Kylian up at the airport in a flashy car? Kylian froze and asked: "Should I take my shoes off?"

"Of course not," laughed Zizou, "get in."

Kylian was still in a daze as they drove to the training ground. "I was just thinking to myself, I am in Zizou's car," he said. "I am Kylian from Bondy. This is not real. I must still be sleeping on the airplane."

And guess what? Kylian even met Ronaldo!

The superstar put his arm round Kylian and gave a thumbs-up. Kylian, who was wearing a Real Madrid tracksuit top, took the photo back to his bedroom in Bondy and put it on the wall.

Naturally, next came the seats in the directors' box. For a match against Espanyol the club made sure he and his family had the best seats in the house.

This was Real Madrid's way of trying to impress Kylian and his family. They wanted to sign him straight away. Zidane and Ronaldo had watched Kylian train for a whole week and they knew he would be a big star.

Kylian's mum and dad, however, wanted him to stay at school and remain close to friends and family in France. They felt that staying at school, playing at Bondy under the watchful eye of his father and being able to play with his friends would help him stay healthy, happy and focused.

## Chelsea Trial

When he was eleven Kylian had had a trial at Chelsea. It began a period of Kylian begging his parents to let him leave for a big club in a big city.

His eyes had been opened to possibilities and he was hungry to improve his football education in a foreign country. But his mum and dad knew what was best for him. He had to stay patient.

Kylian had spent a week with Chelsea and he played for their Under-12s team against Charlton, alongside Tammy Abraham, who would go on to play for England. Poor Charlton didn't know what hit them. "I think we won seven or eight nil," Kylian said.

In fact, it was 8–0. Chelsea presented him with a number 10 shirt with KYLIAN on the back. He met Carlo Ancelotti, one of the best football managers ever. He also met Didier Drogba and Florent Malouda, taking pictures on his dad's phone. His Bondy teammates were amazed when they saw the pictures.

But despite his excellent performance, Chelsea asked Kylian to return for another trial. Kylian's mum was furious. She thought that they should have been able to recognise how good a player he was going to be in a week of training. She said they should have made an immediate offer. This turned out for the best, of course, for Kylian – but not Chelsea, who must regret their decision!

As Kylian's time at Clairefontaine was coming to an end, Chelsea still wanted him, but so did every major club in the world, including all the French clubs, Manchester United, Manchester City, Liverpool, Bayern Munich, and, of course, Real. At fifteen, everyone was talking about the boy wonder from Bondy who had amazing skills and speed. It was decision time for Kylian and his family. Which club would win the race for his signature? Amazingly, he almost signed for a club few people had even heard of.

# THE RACE IS ON

Everyone agreed that stardom beckoned for Kylian when he graduated from Clairefontaine – his coaches, his fellow students, the hundreds of scouts that came to watch him. But Kylian had known it since he was a small boy, so he wasn't worried about finding the right club. He put his faith in his parents.

That's why if they had told him to go to Caen, he would have done. Caen? Who are they? Exactly. They were a small club in Normandy, 125 miles from Paris. They had never won Ligue 1 or even a French cup competition. It was about as unfashionable a club as you can imagine.

When the club contacted Wilfried, Kylian's dad thought it was a joke. "You are trying to catch a whale with a fishing rod," he said.

But Caen knew all about Kylian. They had been watching him since he was twelve, knew his game inside out and knew how to improve him. Unlike most clubs in the race to sign Kylian, Caen had put together a detailed kick-by-kick plan for his career. Wilfried was impressed, and after discussing it as a family, they agreed they would meet with Caen. This was in the early stages of Kylian's Clairefontaine education, when he was thirteen.

Caen told the Mbappés that they would guarantee Kylian would be playing first-team football at the age of sixteen. His father was really pleased – he thought it was crucial for his son's development to play top-flight football as quickly as possible so he could learn to adapt and grow stronger. Indeed, he was so impressed that after a second meeting, they agreed to a deal with Caen before his time at Clairefontaine was up.

However, the move had to be delayed because French league rules meant that clubs couldn't sign young players more than thirty miles from their home. Instead, Kylian would complete his education at Clairefontaine and then join Caen.

## Caen Lose Out

It wasn't to be, though, for the small club. They were denied the chance to sign him after they were relegated from Ligue 1 in 2012. Wilfried agreed that if Caen gained promotion the very next season, Kylian would still sign. But they failed and their chance was gone.

Caen falling out of the race put Rennes at the front. They were not a big club with lots of expensive players, but they did have Kylian's brother, Jirès.

Jirès told Kylian that they could play together and score loads of goals and have even more fun in the red shirts of Rennes. Kylian had a trial at the club and, of course, they were desperate to sign him. And he was keen, too, because it was a club which felt like home. From the age of seven he had been in and around the Rennes training ground and players, looking up to his big brother.

It soon became clear to Real Madrid and the other big European clubs that the Mbappé family wanted

Kylian to stay in France and join a club which would be able to fast-track him into the first team. At clubs such as Real and Manchester United, it could be years before he got close to the first team because of the way these clubs used the transfer system. If they had a hole in the team they filled it by signing a player for millions. That was what was required for a team to stay at the top. Rarely did they have the opportunity to let a young player grow.

So Kylian's dream of playing for Real would not be realised. "Maybe later in your career," said his mum.

Instead, Kylian agreed to join AS Monaco, signing a three-year youth contract at the age of fourteen before his time would be up at Clairefontaine a year later. AS Monaco was a club with a rich tradition for developing France's best players. It had an academy which was very similar to Clairefontaine, their scouts knew the Mbappé family well and it was where Thierry Henry had started too!

# FOOTBALLER FACTORY

AS Monaco was the ideal place for Kylian to develop, and the perfect stepping stone towards realising his ambition.

For a start, he could stay in France and be close to friends and family. Moving to Madrid, to a new city where he didn't know anyone, would have felt like an extra complication.

Most important was the AS Monaco youth academy. It was called La Turbie and it had better facilities than some of the biggest clubs in the world.

Monaco have always taken youth football seriously. In 1987 Arsène Wenger, the famous Arsenal manager, went there and brought to the first team Thierry Henry, Emmanuel Petit and Lilian Thuram. All won the World Cup in 1998, the year Kylian was born. David Trezeguet, the France striker who scored sixty-two goals in 125 matches for his country, was also a Monaco academy graduate. Thierry, Emmanuel and Lilian had joined at the age of fifteen and all played at least 100 matches for Monaco before moving to another team.

With Monaco being such a small place – it has only around 38,000 people living there – the club does not have loads of youngsters in the area to scout. But they have more scouts in the whole of France than any other club, and, amazingly, more scouts in Paris than Paris Saint-Germain. So Monaco knew all about Kylian before anybody else and their scouts were talking with his mum and dad from when he was very young.

Like Caen, Monaco had a plan for Kylian. They would make sure he was fast-tracked into the Under-17s team, and from there he would play for Monaco B. This was Monaco's reserve team. It was proper men's football. Monaco B played in an amateur league but it was a great place for youngsters to get used to the physical side of the sport.

They also had made plans for Kylian to continue his schooling. Monaco employed their own teachers who would visit the club's stadium to hold lessons.

Wilfried was also able to move to Monaco to help his son settle in. The club found father and son a place to live near the training ground while Fayza stayed in Bondy to look after Ethan, who was seven at the time.

When Kylian signed for Monaco, they were a club trying to compete with some of the biggest and richest clubs in the world in the transfer market. Claudio Ranieri, the manager who would later lead Leicester City to their unbelievable Premier League title, was in charge, and thanks to the Russian billionaire owner, Dmitry Rybolovlev, they signed famous players. They wanted to end a thirteen-year wait for the French title.

It was a slight change from their usual style of relying on youngsters. They wanted to blend established superstars with their young talent which was coming through, such as Anthony Martial, who would go on to play for Manchester United. But the club wanted to see what would happen and they knew they had a crop of exciting talent – like Kylian – who would ensure they switched back to their traditions.

Colombian strikers Radamel Falcao and James

Rodríguez had been paired together to score the goals to challenge Paris Saint-Germain in Ligue 1. João Moutinho, the Portugal midfielder, arrived from Porto and his international teammate, the defender Ricardo Carvalho, also signed. France international Eric Abidal, another defender, joined from Barcelona.

Kylian was excited to get going. He and his father discussed what he should try to achieve when at Monaco. They decided he should be in the first team by the end of his three-year youth contract, that he would work hard at school and improve his game. Kylian also added an extra goal for his career at the club: to win Ligue 1. But despite his talent and reputation, Kylian's Monaco career did not get off to a good start.

## Frustration

Despite all the planning by his mum and dad, the detailed career path mapped out by Monaco, the hard work of his coaches at Clairefontaine and, of course, his amazing ability, Kylian suffered his first problem in his career in the early days at La Turbie.

The problem seemed to come from one of the

promises that Monaco had made when he signed: that Kylian would go straight into the Under-17s. The coach of the Under-17s, Bruno Irles, did not agree and said that Kylian was not ready. He was in disagreement with the people who ran the club.

Irles thought the Monaco board should not be telling him how to do his job and so was perhaps harder on Kylian than he might have been on players of a similar age. Irles said Kylian did not track back enough to get the ball back in matches. All he wanted to do was go on mazy runs and score goals.

To help him try to learn that lesson, Irles said he wouldn't play him and instead said he should go to play in an amateur league to understand how his game needed to develop if he was going to make it at the top level. It was a shock for Kylian. How had it come to this? The move to Monaco, following in the footsteps of Thierry Henry, was supposed to be perfect. And yet here he was, not even being allowed to play for the youth team he had signed for?

## Arsenal Calling

Wilfried was angry because he knew what was happening. He had worked in football for so long and had seen it before. Kylian was caught in the middle of this argument between the coach and the board. Irles was using Kylian to make his point. Wilfried would not stand for it and had a row with Irles. Irles insisted he was just trying to help Kylian improve and he wouldn't pick him until he worked harder on the pitch.

With Kylian increasingly unhappy, Wilfried spoke to the Monaco board. Kylian was brought back from the amateur league and with Irles still refusing to play him, his first season at Monaco ended with him training on his own. It was a disaster.

These days, football insiders believe it was all a clever ploy from Monaco to make Kylian hungrier. They wanted him to feel as if he had worked extra hard. Sure, they knew he had the talent but did he have the desire to go with it? By holding him back they thought they were helping. It sure was a risky policy.

Still, with the football world so small, word soon got out that Kylian was unhappy at Monaco. This led to a number of clubs trying to sign Kylian.

The one club which came closest to taking advantage of Kylian's situation was Arsenal. Arsène Wenger had been alerted.

By the time Wenger spoke to Kylian, things were going much better at Monaco but the legendary Arsenal manager still talks about the one that got away. Wenger met with Kylian and his parents at his home in Bondy in a bid to try to persuade him to leave Monaco and there was even talk of a transfer fee of £230,000. It was low because of rules concerning young players. That would have been one of the biggest bargains in football history.

## Monaco's Star Factory – How They Do It

**Scouting:** Monaco have more scouts than any other team in France, and they are the most qualified. They track players from the age of eleven.

**Play everywhere:** Youngsters are played in lots of different positions to help them understand the game more. They do this until they are seventeen.

**Smartphones:** As soon as a match has finished youth players are sent feedback about their performance on their smartphone.

**Monaco B:** This is Monaco's reserve team. It is a mix of older professional players and the best youngsters. They play in France's fourth league, the highest amateur division. The team gives young players a taste of the physicality of men's football.

# BACK TO HIS BEST

Kylian's second season at Monaco was much better, largely because the coach who didn't think he was good enough, Bruno Irles, had left. Instead, Kylian was coached by Frédéric Barilaro. Barilaro had no such doubts about Kylian's ability and attitude.

With his confidence restored Kylian was back to his best. He dazzled in the youth teams to the extent that it was decided he should be promoted to the Under-19s team. He ran off the ball to make space for others. He tracked back. He passed when he should pass. He dribbled when he should dribble. And the goals flowed as his finishing skills improved …

BANG! In one match he cleverly darted between the two central defenders, allowed a pass to come across his body and with his right foot he shot it past the keeper.

ZOOM! In another he picked the ball up on the left-winger, outpaced a defender, did a clever stepover to fool another and from a tight angle squeezed the ball into the net.

DINK! Taking a cross from the left Kylian again let the ball roll across his body and with the outside of his right foot he chipped the ball past the despairing dive of the goalkeeper.

All goals were celebrated in the style of his idol, Cristiano Ronaldo – a jump in the air and as he landed, bringing his arms down from a cross position to his sides as if to say, "GAME OVER!"

Kylian's return to form was perfect timing. Monaco had stopped spending big transfer fees on players. Their plan to take on Paris Saint-Germain had failed. The best they had managed was a second-placed finish behind the Paris giants in that 2013–14 season. They were going to need their starlets instead, and one of them in particular. But first they had to persuade him to stay.

## Breakthrough

At the start of the 2015–16 season Kylian was sixteen years old. Remember that Caen had promised he would be playing first-team football at that age? Kylian and his family had not forgotten. They were worried that Monaco would not give him a chance in the new campaign.

More big clubs were showing an interest in signing Kylian, particularly after the family's meeting with Arsène Wenger. Paris Saint-Germain were interested. RB Leipzig, the German club, had also emerged as a possible destination. But Kylian and his dad decided that if Kylian left early he could earn a reputation for being a difficult character. They were also aware that if he joined a new club he would have to start from scratch. Trusted family advisors had also warned that the first-team environment at a new club would be harsh. Kylian was still an unknown and senior pros wouldn't give him the time of day.

His brother Jirès had given him advice too: work harder, improve your game, score goals and everything will work out. Well, to Kylian that was easy. He decided to play so well that Monaco would have to pick him for first-team action. He wasted little time in making an impact, scoring ten goals in his first five matches that season for the Under-19s team.

The club's vice president Vadim Vasilyev came to watch Kylian in training. He couldn't believe his eyes. Everything that he had been told was true: Monaco had a goalscoring wonderkid, one with speed, skill and a burning desire to do well.

He immediately set up a meeting with Wilfried and Fayza as he was keen to reassure them that Kylian was a big part of the club's future. They pointed out that Kylian had to be playing first-team football by the end of his three-year youth contract, otherwise they would have to seriously consider moving him. Vasilyev, desperate not to lose their star asset, said, "No problem, he will train with the first team as soon as possible."

When Kylian first stepped on to the training pitch with the first team, he knew his time had come. This was no time to be nervous or afraid. He had to show them what he could do.

Everything clicked for Kylian in that training session. He outpaced all the defenders. He tracked back. He didn't give the ball away. He finished like a player at his peak. It was such a brilliant performance that it was talked about for weeks at the club and it has not been forgotten to this day.

Leonardo Jardim, the first-team manager, also couldn't believe what he had seen. "This boy must not go back to the reserves," he said. Jardim claimed him as one of his own. Kylian was a first-team player now.

It would take only another month before Jardim unleashed Kylian Mbappé on the professional football world. But few who saw it would have predicted how he was going to take the world by storm after a low-key debut on a chilly Wednesday night in December 2015.

There were only a few thousand fans in Monaco's home stadium, the Stade Louis II, for the match against Caen, the club which had come close to signing Kylian from Clairefontaine.

Monaco had been winning the game 1–0 until the eighty-sixth minute when Caen managed an equaliser. Jardim thought it was the ideal time to try Kylian. It was a low-pressure game, the defenders were tired, and if he put Kylian on the young man would be a record breaker.

With eighteen days to go until his seventeenth birthday, Kylian would be the youngest ever to don the famous red and white shirt of Monaco. The previous holder of the record? Thierry Henry. Monaco and Kylian both wanted this record to change hands. For Monaco, it would further improve their reputation as a club which produced excellent talent. For Kylian, well, he always knew he was going to be a record breaker.

And so in the eighty-eighth minute Kylian was told, "It's time." He took off his tracksuit, after doing some quick sprints down the touchline to warm up, and waited for Fábio Coentrão to shake hands with him before Fabio came off and Kylian replaced him. Kylian was told to try to cause as much damage as possible.

In the end he got few touches on the ball. He had one dangerous run which Caen did well to halt with a well-timed tackle. It was a glimpse of the blistering speed which would soon be terrorising defenders. Kylian knew it was just the start. He left the field disappointed, though, wishing he had scored and that Monaco had won the match.

## Scaring Spurs

For Monaco's next match, against Bastia, Kylian had to make do with a place on the bench again. With the match in the balance, Jardim was reluctant to risk him and he didn't go on. Monaco scored twice in the last eighteen minutes to take the win.

But he did come off the bench in their next match. It was away to Tottenham Hotspur in the Europa League, the sort of occasion that Kylian had dreamed of being involved in and knew he belonged at. He came on after fifty-six minutes with Monaco 3–0 down. He needed five minutes to make an impact.

When he was passed the ball on the left wing, Kylian immediately had the full-back back-pedalling furiously. He turned his rival inside out with two magical stepovers, and with the Tottenham defence keen to get two players to tackle him he had managed to do something his coaches had always told him to think about: find space for others. With Tottenham panicking, Kylian's sharp pass found Stephan El Shaarawy, who curled a brilliant shot into the net.

The full-back, by the way, was Kieran Trippier,

who would go on to star for England in the 2018 World Cup.

For the rest of the match Kylian was a constant threat with fast, direct running and tricks. On that performance he should have been playing from the start. Manager Jardim didn't disagree. In Monaco's next match but one, away to Bordeaux, Kylian was in the starting XI. But it was a bad day for the team as they lost 3–0, although Kylian once again gave notice that he was dangerous.

Kylian had made a strong impression, but Jardim wanted him to do more work on his game with the reserves. He was told that there was no rush and they planned to bring him back into the squad in a few games' time. Kylian worked harder than ever before and he was back on the substitutes bench against Toulouse in January 2016. Both Monaco and Kylian had an eye on another record: Monaco's youngest ever goalscorer.

## History Boy

In the third match after his return to the first team, Kylian made history. Monaco were winning

2–1 against Troyes. Kylian had come on in the seventy-third minute. He had been as electric as ever and the Monaco fans were now well aware they had someone very special to cheer on. The clock had ticked over into the ninety-third minute. Troyes were pushing for an equalising goal but carelessly gave the ball away, letting Hélder Costa run towards goal. He crossed from the left and there were two Monaco players racing to meet the ball … Kylian and Tiémoué Bakayoko.

But Tiémoué didn't have Kylian's pace and he couldn't match his desire for his first goal. Kylian sprinted to connect with the pass and without slowing down or steadying himself, struck a perfect left-footed shot over the helpless keeper into the net. YES! Kylian Mbappé had arrived. And smashed another record. He was Monaco's youngest ever goalscorer at the age of seventeen years and sixty-two days, beating, you guessed it, Thierry Henry.

He was so happy, Kylian ran off with his arms stretched out like a plane. He felt like he was flying. His teammates came over to hug him. After the congratulations, Kylian did a cool dance and gave a thumbs-up to the crowd.

For the rest of the season, Kylian started one more match (against Nantes) and made five more substitute appearances, including away to Paris Saint-Germain in a brilliant 2–0 win for Monaco. It helped Monaco to finish third in the 2015–16 season and ensure they qualified for the Champions League – and that was crucial in helping to persuade Kylian to sign for Monaco again.

On 7 March 2016 Kylian agreed a three-year contract. His first proper professional deal. Club president Vadim Vasilyev said Kylian was "a player of great talent".

He was right, of course. And Monaco's timing was perfect, not just because the big clubs were trying to convince him to leave. That summer Kylian would boost his reputation further.

# EURO STAR

A lot had happened in a short space of time for Kylian. He had established himself as a first-team squad member at Monaco and signed his first professional contract. This was no surprise to those who knew about French football. His name was known. In the summer of 2016, he made sure the whole of Europe knew who he was.

Kylian was the star of the European Under-19 Championship in Germany. He produced sizzling performances which are still talked about. One European football scout said: "He bossed the whole tournament."

But he almost didn't play. Despite success at academies and his clubs, Kylian had rarely represented France's youth teams. He had played twice for the Under-17s. The Under-18s coach, Jean-Claude Giuntini, seemed to have a grudge against Kylian and said he didn't work hard enough for the team.

It was strange because most coaches who worked with Kylian and most scouts who watched him all reported that his attitude was flawless. Unfortunately, though, the opinions of a tiny number of coaches, and that difficult start at Monaco, had denied him matches for France. He had, amazingly, been left out of the France squad for the European Under-17 Championship in 2015, a tournament they won.

Unsurprisingly, the seventeen-year-old Kylian wasted little time in proving his doubters wrong. He was a key player as France qualified for the tournament when they needed to win their last three matches. He was full of wonderful running and mazy dribbling in a victory over Montenegro. He then scored in a 4–0 beating of Denmark.

In the final match, against Serbia, the pressure was on. France had to win.

Kylian was everywhere. He played on the right

wing. He played on the left. Both full-backs were given a difficult time. He picked up the ball in central midfield and tried to play the strikers through on goal. He had a shot cleared off the line. At times he was playing them on his own. So it was no surprise he hit the winning goal, just before half-time.

Jean-Kévin Augustin, the striker, played a neat pass to Kylian on the right-hand side of the area. Kylian shimmied, found space and unleashed a shot which beat the goalkeeper at his near post. Brilliant.

Jean-Kévin and Kylian combining would be a sign of things to come. Coach Batelli knew he had a special duo on his hands.

France were one of the favourites to win the tournament, which was held in Germany. But their campaign got off to a bad start when they were beaten 2–1 by England. Kylian was subbed off in the second half as he struggled with England's physicality. Jean-Kévin scored the goal for France.

In the next match, however, both Kylian and Jean-Kévin were on the scoresheet as they beat Croatia 2–0. It was the start of Jean-Kévin and Kylian having their own personal goalscoring battle. Who could score most?

The final group match was one France could not afford to lose. There was no danger of that, though, as Kylian and Jean-Kévin ran riot. Kylian scored twice but Jean-Kévin notched one more for a hat-trick! France qualified for the semi-finals in second position from their group, behind England.

## Destroyer

Kylian took centre stage in the semis against Portugal. He destroyed them on his own, scoring two goals and setting up the other. And all of that after France had gone behind in the third minute.

The equaliser came in the tenth minute. Kylian had the ball near the corner flag on the left wing with two Portugal players surrounding him. *Easy*, he thought. A few tricks and a burst of pace later and he was in the box, squaring the ball for Ludovic Blas to tap home.

Throughout the game Kylian was a menace. His feet were so fast they were a blur and the poor Portuguese defenders couldn't cope. After a flashing stepover one stumbled and fell in a heap. He was beating the Portuguese at will, playing in his teammates for chances and shooting from distance himself.

His two goals were actually rather simple. A tap-in from a right-wing cross and then a cute flicked header from a corner. "He's had a great game," the commentator said. That was an understatement.

In the final against Italy Kylian made gaps for his teammates just by being on the pitch. It was an easy win for France as Jean-Kévin scored the first of four goals. Kylian was desperate to get on the scoresheet but it wasn't to be as his friend pipped him by one goal to end up with six for the tournament.

In the stands watching with his parents was Atmane Airouche, the president of Bondy. He was very proud to see the boy from Bondy shining on such an important stage. But something surprised him.

"We met him outside the stadium and we were shocked that he didn't want to go partying with his teammates," he said. "Instead he wanted to go straight home. To him, he had achieved his goal to be European champion and was already thinking about his next goal: going back to Monaco, getting into their team, winning more titles."

# MONACO MARVEL

Remember when Kylian first signed for Monaco aged fourteen? He didn't just want to break through into the first team, he wanted to win the league title. So as the 2016–17 season began for Monaco, Kylian's head was full of dreams of lifting the trophy. And why not? He had just played for France's Under-19s and was the biggest and brightest young star in Europe.

But Kylian came back to earth with a bump. In Monaco's first match of the season against Guingamp, he suffered a nasty head injury and had to come off. Monaco were losing 2–0 at the time. His replacement,

Bernardo Silva, helped turn the game around and it was Silva who equalised in the eighty-fourth minute.

From then on, Valère Germain was preferred to Kylian as Monaco couldn't stop winning. After the Guingamp match, they won seven matches in a row, including a 2–1 victory over Tottenham in the Champions League. Even Paris Saint-Germain were beaten, in an amazing 3–1 win for Monaco. Kylian didn't even make the squad for those two games and until he returned to the starting XI against Montpellier almost six long weeks later, he had played only twenty-eight minutes off the bench in three games.

Kylian was, of course, frustrated. But he knew it was really hard for a manager to change a winning team, let alone a strike force that was doing so well. Instead he worked harder than ever in training, recognising that in his first full season with the first team there was still plenty to learn.

So when his chance came against Montpellier, Kylian was ready. He won Monaco a penalty. Four minutes into the second half, Kylian showed exactly how hard he had been working with a style of goal that he was not known for, a deft header from a sweeping cross from the right. He had outmuscled the defender to grab a yard of space and leapt high, glancing the ball back into the net. Monaco went on to win the match 6–2.

They didn't look back. Nor did Kylian. Three games later Kylian scored against Nancy. Three games after that he scored against Bastia. He had found his feet in the first team. Monaco's fans were full of praise for their brilliant young striker. Not only was he scoring goals but he was showing pace and skill on the ball. Sooner or later, everyone at Monaco felt, Kylian was going to destroy a team.

## Hat-trick Hero

Poor Rennes would be that team on a Wednesday night in December in the French Cup. After twenty-one minutes, Kylian had secured the match for Monaco, having scored twice. The first goal was a carefully placed left-foot shot from the edge of the area. The second was all about blistering pace. Freed down the left-hand side, Kylian raced towards the goal and sent a shot into the far corner with his right foot. With almost seventy minutes left could he claim his first professional hat-trick?

Absolutely. The third goal arrived in the sixty-first minute and it completed what many onlookers thought was a complete hat-trick, displaying a full range of skills. His first two goals had been about precision and power with left and right foot. This one was cheeky and clever. Played in on goal with the goalkeeper rushing out and defenders lurking, Kylian had to think fast on his feet. He managed to get a right-footed clip away just in time.

As a sign of how much he had grown up, Kylian did not celebrate in the style of his idol Cristiano Ronaldo. He was his own man now. He punched the air and nodded his head as if to say, "This is where I belong!"

Monaco won the match 7–0. It was their seventy-sixth goal in twenty-eight matches. Monaco ended the year on a seemingly unstoppable charge to the league title. Yet Kylian was only just warming up.

In February, after a crucial strike against Montpellier in a 2–1 win, he made history again in the next contest against Metz. Another hat-trick. Kylian had been in devastating form from kick-off but even those who knew of his talent were amazed at how quickly he scored three goals. It only took him fifty minutes. At eighteen years and two months he became the youngest player ever to score a hat-trick in Ligue 1.

In his next seven games, Kylian scored seven goals. And one of them was very special indeed.

# CITY STUNNER

When Kylian and his family were worrying about whether Kylian should move early from Monaco or not, a scout told them that if he walked into a different first-team dressing room they would say, "Who are you?"

Well, after his goalscoring glut every dressing room in Europe knew who Kylian was. He had earned his stripes in men's football and he had proven his doubters wrong.

Monaco coach Leonardo Jardim had been hugely impressed by Kylian's play. So it was time to unleash him from the start on the biggest stage possible: the Champions League.

And against Manchester City no less, managed by the legend that is Pep Guardiola. It is crazy to think that Kylian was only eighteen years old when Jardim pulled him to one side in training in the days before the game and said, "You are starting against Manchester City." Even crazier to think that Kylian was not in the least bit nervous. Instead he told his manager that it was a decision he wouldn't regret.

Earlier in the season Kylian had made two Champions League appearances, but both were off the bench, against CSKA Moscow and Bayer Leverkusen. In Manchester, he would play from the start in one of the biggest stadiums in Europe, in front of more than 50,000 fans and against some of the world's best defenders.

There were still no nerves from Kylian as he and his Monaco teammates took to the pitch. Kylian was desperate to do well and had been told to attack-attack-attack down Manchester City's left side. Coach Jardim thought City were weak there and Kylian would make hay.

He was right. With the game poised at 1–1 after Radamel Falcao had equalised Raheem Sterling's goal, Kylian's pace and positivity brought him a chance. He outpaced the legend Yaya Touré but fired his shot wide. *Next time*, Kylian seemed to be saying to himself. He then bamboozled Nicolás Otamendi with a brilliant turn. Then he fooled the defender again, nutmegging him and leaving him in a heap on the turf.

In the fortieth minute, Kylian gave Monaco a sensational lead. And it was all down to his speed and brains. A clipped pass in behind the City defence looked harmless but Kylian burst through a gap, spinning off the shoulder of poor Nicolás again. Suddenly in a blur, Kylian was in on goal and the ball was in the back of the net.

"MMM-BA-PAY!" screamed the commentator.

At eighteen years and two months Kylian was the second-youngest Frenchman to score in the Champions League. The youngest was Karim Benzema. Not bad company, was it?

Kylian should have had another goal in the second half as City and Monaco traded goals in a thrilling game. It would finish 5–3 to City but Monaco were far from disheartened. They had scored crucial away goals, which would make a difference if the scores were level on aggregate (the total number of goals scored in both games). City were disappointed. And a little afraid. What would Kylian do to them next time?

City were right to be worried. In the second leg it took only six minutes for Kylian to fire a warning shot. Again, from nowhere, he outpaced the City defence, getting in on goal only for goalkeeper Willy Caballero to make a fine save. Less than two minutes later Kylian found the net with a poacher's goal. He instinctively stuck out a leg to turn home Bernardo Silva's smash across goal. Monaco were only a goal behind.

They continued to attack the City goal with Kylian playing brilliantly. In the thirty-first minute they went 2–0 up and made it 5–5 on aggregate with Fabinho slotting home. Even Leroy Sané pulling a goal back and putting City into an overall lead of 6–5 couldn't halt Monaco's charge. They scored again seven minutes later for a 3–1 win on the night and a 6–6 tie over the two legs. Those three goals in Manchester, including Kylian's, were enough for them to progress.

Monaco seemed unstoppable. They were hailed as the most exciting team in the tournament. And Kylian was their driving force. The newspapers, playing catch-up, called him the new Thierry Henry.

France legend Robert Pires was one of the first to compare Kylian to Thierry Henry. "I had the pleasure of playing with Henry and I can tell you he was doing the same things at [Kylian's age]. They're the same players. He's going to keep improving and he'll have a great career."

## The Famous Celebration

In the quarter-finals against German giants Borussia Dortmund, Kylian saw them off on his own. Dortmund were scared of Kylian's pace and he won Monaco a penalty with a burst which left them standing. But oh no! Fabinho missed, his shot going wide of the left-hand post.

It didn't matter, though. Kylian turned in a cross with his thigh to give them the lead in the nineteenth minute. It seemed a lucky goal but Kylian didn't care as he slid across the grass on his knees. "Yes!" he said.

Unfortunately, Monaco's defence made a mistake, even after an own goal had given Monaco a two-goal cushion. It was 2-1 heading into the final stages. Kylian was stalking the Dortmund defence, waiting for any error – and in the seventy-ninth minute they made one. A loose pass was pounced on by Kylian. He could have a clear run on goal if he wanted. Instead he took the ball a few yards and unleashed a shot from outside the area high into the net.

Kylian slid away on his knees and for the first time fans glimpsed what would be an iconic celebration. He folded his arms across his chest as if to say 'job done'. As Kylian had been smashing goals in left, right and centre for months, his younger brother Ethan had told him that Kylian needed to have his own celebration. He was now too famous to be copying Ronaldo's.

But even this wasn't his own – Kylian had borrowed it from Ethan. This was how the kid would celebrate when he scored a goal against his older brother when playing *FIFA*. Kylian liked the celebration, though, because it was a way to show Ethan he was thinking of him even in the biggest games in Europe.

And there would be more to come. In the second leg of the quarter-final, Dortmund were beaten 3–1 with Kylian again on the scoresheet. It set up a

Champions League semi-final with Juventus. Wow. How far had Kylian come in such a short time? He was tingling with excitement as he walked out against the famous Italian team.

But sadly, Juventus were too strong in the first leg at Monaco's ground. Their experienced and hardened players had too many tricks for Monaco's youngsters and they won 2–0. Kylian briefly gave Monaco hope in the second leg with a sixty-ninth-minute goal but it wasn't to be.

*Never mind*, Kylian thought. *One day I will win the Champions League.* It had always been his ambition. But before that, he knew he was more likely to realise his goal of winning the French title. And with six goals in eight games, Kylian was in perfect form to make history.

# TITLE JOY

Paris Saint-Germain had been breathing down their necks in Ligue 1 all season. And Monaco, despite putting together winning runs consistently – they had won eight in a row as a crucial match against Lille approached – couldn't quite shake them off. But they knew if they kept winning, PSG would not catch them.

Lille were tough opponents but if Monaco beat them they would then only have to beat Saint-Étienne, in the second from last game of the season, to confirm the title.

There were no nerves in the Monaco dressing

room. How could there be? They had proved to be one of the best teams in Europe. And they came flying at Lille as soon as the first whistle went. Predictably, Kylian led the way with darting runs. Radamel Falcao scored after only six minutes for a 1–0 lead.

On the stroke of half-time, Kylian put the game beyond doubt with a mazy bit of skill and dribbling to cross for Bernardo Silva. For good measure, Kylian made the third for Radamel as Monaco went on to win 4–0. Now they just needed to beat Saint-Étienne in front of their home crowd to win their first title since 2000, when Kylian was just a year old!

And you just know who scored the opening goal to set Monaco on their way ... Kylian! It was a trademark Kylian goal. A pass through the middle gave the Saint-Étienne defence no chance of keeping up with him. He could have shot first time but instead Kylian thought he'd have some fun and dribble around the goalkeeper. For a second it looked as though he had taken the ball too wide but, cool as you like, he slotted the ball home. And to celebrate? The trademark Kylian celebration at the corner flag, arms across chest and a nod of the head.

Monaco won 2–0 and the title was theirs. Cue

epic celebrations on the pitch in front of a packed stadium! Kylian was ecstatic as he watched the fans celebrating, waving their huge red and white flags.

## The Next Messi

In Monaco's title-winning season, Kylian was scoring or making a goal every sixty-five minutes. Only Lionel Messi had a better record than that in Europe's top five leagues.

## Taking it Easy

Kylian could have gone to a hundred parties that night but instead he went home to be with his family. He wanted to think about what he had achieved. When he arrived at Monaco he said he wanted to be in the first team after three seasons. He was. He also said he wanted to be a Ligue 1 winner. He was.

There were the records and the awards too. When he passed fifteen goals for the season at the age of eighteen years and 147 days, he became the youngest in more than 100 years to manage such a tally in the top divisions of France, England, Germany, Italy and Spain. In league and cups he had scored twenty-six times and made eleven more goals. He was named as the fourth-best forward in Europe by UEFA, with his idol Cristiano Ronaldo winning. He also made the UEFA team of the season and won the Ligue 1 Young Player of the Year award.

A lesser-known achievement was passing his school exams! Kylian earned a qualification in management of science and technology. It was just as he promised his parents. When Kylian put his mind to something, on the pitch or not, he achieved.

His joy was tinged with sadness, though, because he knew he might be leaving Monaco.

All the biggest clubs in the world positioned themselves on the starting line in the race to sign Kylian. And the price was about to go up.

# LES BLEUS

Kylian could have played international football for Cameroon because that's where his dad was from. Or he could have chosen Algeria because of his mum. A boy in a hurry could easily have been swayed by the certainty that both of those countries would have made him one of the youngest international players ever. Either would have been the easy, quick fix. But Kylian wasn't interested in doing things the easy way.

France was the only country he wanted to represent. And he didn't just want to play for Les Bleus, he wanted to star for them and win European

Championships and World Cups. Those were his goals. As he always said to his father, "You have to aim as high as possible."

Didier Deschamps, the France manager, loved this attitude. So as soon as he got the chance to pick Kylian, he did. In March 2017 Kylian was named in the senior squad. This was instead of going to the Under-20 World Cup with France in South Korea. He immediately wowed more experienced teammates. Olivier Giroud couldn't believe how mature and confident he was.

Kylian made his debut against Luxembourg on 25 March, coming off the bench. At eighteen years, three months and five days he was the second-youngest ever to play for his country. Another record. But he was disappointed that day – he should have scored with his first touch of the ball, the goalkeeper pulling off a brilliant save.

Too fast!

Three days later he started his first match for France. And against the mighty Spain, no less. He had some good moments in the game, showing signs of his speed and skills, but it was in his second start that he really impressed – against England in a friendly in

June. This was the game when Monaco began to add extra millions to his transfer price.

Kylian tormented England alongside fellow youth star Ousmane Dembélé. But no one should have been surprised. In the England defence that day was Manchester City's John Stones, whom Kylian had outplayed in those famous games for Monaco in the Champions League. Kieran Trippier, someone Kylian had fooled against Tottenham Hotspur early in his career, was also playing. Kylian was too fast, too positive and too tricky – in one dribble he did a stepover so quickly that Kieran almost fell over!

Kylian hit the bar and had a certain goal denied by goalkeeper Tom Heaton, who stuck out a right leg to stop the ball nestling in the corner. France won 3–2. The margin of victory would have been bigger had Raphaël Varane not been sent off.

It was a significant performance from Kylian coming against England. Sure, they were not an international powerhouse, but as one of the most famous teams, people took notice. The big English clubs like Arsenal, Liverpool and Manchester United needed no further proof Kylian was the real deal. They all wanted him, but there were only two clubs in the race and one was in pole position.

# THIS TIME FOR REAL?

On a swelteringly hot Monaco summer's day in 2017, a luxurious private jet waited on the tarmac to fly the second-most expensive footballer of all time to join his new teammates on a pre-season tour in Miami. Real Madrid thought they had their man. The Spanish giants were putting the final touches on a deal which would see them unite Kylian and his idol, Cristiano Ronaldo, in the famous white strip.

The fee would be £161 million. Monaco had reluctantly agreed to sell. They knew they couldn't keep Kylian forever and the Madrid offer was far too big to turn down. Amazingly, though, there was a problem, one which few could have predicted: Kylian didn't want to join Real.

Despite admitting that playing for Real was one of his goals, despite the chance to play alongside Ronaldo and despite the prospect of a Champions League winner's medal, Kylian said there was no need for the plane. What had happened?

Firstly, Kylian had not been convinced that he would play every week. When he was speaking to coach Zinedine Zidane, Kylian was surprised to be told that Ronaldo, Karim Benzema, the France striker, and Gareth Bale would still be the preferred front three. The prospect of being frustrated and angry in Madrid, a long way from his family, meant Kylian said no.

Did this let in the likes of Liverpool, Manchester United and Arsenal? Well, Kylian's dad spoke to them all. But going to England was never a realistic option. Wilfried was just being smart by understanding exactly what Kylian's options were.

Instead, it was Paris Saint-Germain who held all the cards. And in fact, they had done for a long, long time. The key was Wilfried's friendship with

Marc Westerloppe, PSG's head of recruitment. Westerloppe had known Wilfried for years and Kylian's dad trusted him so much he had almost arranged for his son to sign for RC Lens when he was younger because Westerloppe worked there.

## "Come and Join Me"

Westerloppe set up a meeting at Kylian's family home on 7 July. Unai Emery, the PSG manager, was there and assured Kylian that he would be first choice. They told him that he would likely be playing alongside Neymar, the brilliant Brazil forward. PSG were also in talks to sign him from Barcelona.

Kylian remained unsure, however. He was excited about the prospect of a new season with Monaco. They had such great players! Maybe he could win the Champions League with them? PSG didn't give up. In fact, once they had signed Neymar they told him to send Kylian text messages. "Come and join me! We will score loads of goals."

In the end, Monaco took the decision out of Kylian's hands. They had financial worries and needed the money. They had also sold Bernardo Silva and Benjamin Mendy to Manchester City. Monaco's amazing team was being broken up.

As pre-season began, PSG agreed an initial loan deal so they would not break financial fair play rules. They would pay £122 million with another £40 million due in bonuses. Kylian would earn more than £18 million a year, the highest salary ever for an eighteen-year-old.

## Most Expensive Footballers

**Neymar:** Barcelona to Paris Saint-Germain €222m 2017

**Kylian Mbappé:** Monaco to Paris Saint-Germain €185m 2017

**João Félix:** Benfica to Atlético Madrid €126m 2019

**Philippe Coutinho:** Liverpool to Barcelona €160m 2018

> **Antoine Griezmann:** Atlético Madrid to Barcelona €120m 2019

Kylian's big move was announced in the final few hours of that summer's transfer window. It also happened to be the day that Kylian would score his first international goal, against Holland in Paris.

When he was unveiled as a PSG player six days after that goal against the Netherlands, he said: "It was important for me to stay in France. I wanted to come back home, to the town where I grew up. With hard work we'll be able to achieve our goal of winning lots of trophies, including the club's ultimate dream: the Champions League."

# THE MCN

Before Monaco's Kylian-inspired stunning title success, Paris Saint-Germain had been the all-conquering force in French football. They had won the league for four years in a row. It was a no-brainer for them to sign Kylian. With one cheque they strengthened themselves and weakened their nearest challengers.

And with another cheque, they had done the same to their European rivals. Neymar's arrival from Barcelona was a clear sign of intent and motivated by revenge. Barcelona had humiliated PSG in the Champions League the previous season. They had to add the Champions League to their domestic success. A strike force of Kylian, Neymar and Edinson Cavani, the striker from Uruguay, was one of the most fearsome ever seen. They would be known as 'the MCN'.

Unsurprisingly, the MCN wasted little time in proving that they would be too good for their French rivals. By the time Kylian made his debut five games into the season against Metz, PSG had won their first four games and scored fourteen goals. PSG would win thirteen of their first fifteen league games. Naturally, Kylian scored on his debut.

PSG also started the Champions League in blistering form. They beat Scottish giants Celtic 5–0 in their first game of the qualifying group in Glasgow with Kylian on the scoresheet. It was merely a warning shot to the rest of the continent. Bayern Munich were dismissed 3–0 in Paris, Celtic were again thrashed out of sight 7–1 (Kylian scored again) while Anderlecht were beaten 9–0 on aggregate.

At Christmas, PSG were top of Ligue 1. They had a nine-point gap to Monaco, in second place. The strike force of Kylian, Neymar and Edinson had scored thirty-eight goals between them.

They were also through to the round of sixteen

of the Champions League, despite a loss to Bayern in the final group game. PSG's MCN had scored twenty-five times in six games. Kylian had scored PSG's only goal in the Bayern loss but had taken away another record – at eighteen years, eleven months and five days he became the youngest player to score ten Champions League goals. The record had previously belonged to Karim Benzema of Real Madrid.

And guess which team PSG were drawn against in their next match? Real, the twelve-time Champions League winners.

## Face to Face with His Idol

It was a match which the whole world was excited about. Two of the most powerful clubs in Europe, plus the added spice of Kylian going up against the team which had come so close to signing him in the summer and his first on-pitch meeting with his hero, Cristiano Ronaldo. But as the media whipped themselves into a frenzy about the clash, Kylian did not play along. In fact, quite the opposite. He said: "I loved him when I was little but that is finished." Wow. He meant business.

And he had to. It didn't get much bigger than a Champions League knockout match at the intimidating Bernabéu. There were almost 80,000 packed into the famous stadium. Was Kylian nervous? No chance. After all, he'd been to the Bernabéu as a boy and it was Real who had been so desperate to sign him. He had never felt so confident.

Kylian was revelling playing on such an important stage. The defenders were wary of him and a hush came over the crowd when he got the ball because the Real fans were scared too. And at twenty-one minutes he showed why. Picking up the ball on the right, Kylian found space for a wicked cross, which was eventually met by Adrien Rabiot, who found the net.

Real equalised through a Ronaldo penalty but Kylian almost restored the lead twice. He had a rasping shot saved and then was inches away from connecting with a left-field cross. He slid on the turf but couldn't reach the ball for a tap-in. So close!

Unfortunately PSG lost concentration. In the last eight minutes they not only conceded once but twice. It was a disaster. They had given Real a two-goal start in the second leg.

The MCN remained confident. *If anyone can*

*do it, it's us.* For the first half, PSG threatened but Real's defence stood firm. Kylian was the first to break through just before half-time. But instead of squaring the ball to Cavani who had an easy tap-in, Kylian chose to shoot. Saved! He buried his face in his hands. It was a reminder that even Kylian could make a mistake and set the tone for the game as Real went on to win 2–1.

PSG did win the league title easily, though. Their total silverware haul included the Coupe de France, Coupe de la Ligue and Trophée des Champions. Kylian scored twenty-one goals in forty-three games in that domestic treble, earning him another Ligue 1 Young Player of the Year award and the Golden Boy trophy. At home, and in Europe, Kylian had proved he was ready for the grandest stage of all: the World Cup Finals.

# WATCH OUT WORLD

There was never any doubt that Kylian would be named in France's twenty-three-man squad to go to Russia to try to win a second World Cup. But Kylian didn't want to leave it to chance.

In a friendly match against Russia in Moscow, he made sure he would be on that plane. He scored twice. The second was a brilliant goal. Kylian dribbled into the left-hand side of the Russian penalty area and, in a blur, dragged the ball over his heel, flashed two stepovers to make space for the shot and fired home at the near post. Coach Didier Deschamps had seen enough. He took Kylian off – why risk an injury at this stage? – and gave him a congratulatory hug.

France's strength in depth was revealed when the squad was named. There was no room for Karim Benzema or Alexandre Lacazette. Kylian was, of course, included. He was ecstatic. "My first World Cup! My dream!" he said on social media. Best of all, he was given the number 10 shirt. This was a huge honour as it was the same number that Zinedine Zidane had worn

Being part of a World Cup squad was like nothing Kylian had experienced before. When they arrived at their hotel in Istra, Moscow, the hotel staff clapped and cheered. They were each given a Russian doll and the doors to their room had been personalised with painted images of them. Kylian's showed him punching the air. His huge bed had his name on and there were pictures of Kylian playing for France on the walls. They had also been given PlayStations!

In the first game against Australia, Kylian had to pinch himself about what was happening. In the tunnel he looked over at Ousmane Dembélé. They smiled at each other and shook their heads.

Kylian said to him: "Look at us. The boy from

Évreux and the boy from Bondy. We are playing at the World Cup."

"I swear, it's unbelievable," said Ousmane

Kylian walked out onto the pitch and said he felt he had 65 million French people behind him. When he heard 'La Marseillaise', the French national anthem, he almost cried.

## Work Harder

France did not start the tournament with the performance they wanted. They beat Australia 2–1 but had needed an eightieth-minute own goal to win. Didier Deschamps, the manager, was furious. And one player in particular had angered him: Kylian!

Deschamps called a team meeting to discuss the performance. He said that Australia's players had worked harder, run further and ran faster. Australia did twice as many sprints as France's players and Kylian had done fewest of anybody. "I thought speed was your strength," Deschamps said to Kylian.

Kylian said he would do better. He wouldn't make

the same error again. Deschamps made sure of that too. In training he was on Kylian's case constantly: track back, make space for others, use your left foot, don't give the ball away. But Kylian didn't mind. He knew Deschamps was just trying to help him and he loved him for it. He would say of his coach: "I would die on the pitch for him."

In the next match against Peru, Kylian made amends. His thirty-fourth-minute goal was enough for the victory. It was another record! The youngest France player to score at a major tournament!

It wasn't a fluent performance from France but few could complain with two wins from two matches. It meant that in their final match against Denmark, victory was not essential. Deschamps decided to rest players, including Kylian, for the knockout matches to come. They played out a dull 0–0 draw. The France fans in the stadium were furious. They booed the players at full time and the media were critical of Deschamps. France were boring and predictable. Why weren't they thrashing teams when they had such exciting players like Kylian, Antoine Griezmann and Paul Pogba?

Deschamps knew what he was doing, though. He

was making sure the team were organised and the players were tracking back. There would come a time to unleash their full potential – and that time was against Argentina in the last sixteen.

## Destroying Argentina

It was a blockbuster of a match! Two former World Champions going head to head for a place in the quarter-finals. And Kylian versus Lionel Messi. The boy who would be king against the thirty-one-year-old master.

Kylian and his French teammates were pumped up. Before the game Paul Pogba had given an inspiring speech. "I am not going home tonight!" he shouted. "I am NOT going home!"

Deschamps had reminded Kylian that speed was his greatest asset. Their defenders were not fast enough to stop him, he said. Deschamps was right.

As soon as he got the chance Kylian attacked them with speed. He tried to get right through the middle of the defence but two Argentina players brought him down as he was about to go into the penalty area. The resulting free kick almost brought a goal – Antoine Griezmann smashing a shot against the bar.

Kylian hit top speed minutes later. He picked the ball up outside France's penalty area and had only one thing on his mind: a goal! He flashed past three Argentina players immediately. Kylian was going all the way! They gave chase but could not get near him. Kylian then zoomed past a fourth player, Marcos Rojo. Marcos couldn't catch him and so as Kylian entered the Argentina box, he fouled him. Penalty!

Antoine scored to give France the lead but the tone had been set for the game. Argentina were scared of Kylian. And why not? That run for the penalty was later timed at 37kph, which was as fast as Usain Bolt. Every time he got the ball he threatened them so they fouled him. It disrupted France's play and two goals either side of half-time gave Argentina an unlikely lead.

France did not panic, though. Eleven minutes later they were level with a brilliant strike from full-back Benjamin Pavard. Argentina were beginning to tire. Kylian sensed his chance.

The goal that gave France the lead would have

been nothing more than a half-chance to most ordinary players. But Kylian's quick feet wrong-footed the defenders in a packed penalty box after he controlled a cross. The space he found gave the chance to shoot. Bang! Into the net from a tight angle. France led 3–2!

Kylian's destruction of Argentina's World Cup dreams was complete four minutes later. Olivier Giroud passed across the box to Kylian, who was approaching at top speed. He hit it first time. Goal!

The world was stunned by the nineteen-year-old's performance. "Watch out world, there's a new number ten!" screamed football commentators, pointing out that Lionel Messi also wears the number. "Mbappé destroys Argentina!" "The boy wonder! He's going to be a world beater."

Those two goals made Kylian the first teenager to score twice in a World Cup game since a seventeen-year-old Pelé in 1958. The Brazilian legend tweeted: "Congratulations, @KMbappe. 2 goals in a World Cup so young puts you in great company!"

## On to the Final

In the quarter-final against Uruguay, Deschamps made sure France returned to a more disciplined way of playing. Uruguay were so concerned about Kylian that just his presence on the pitch made space for others. France won 2–0. It was a comfortable win rather than a spectacular one.

Kylian did not score and was not as threatening but he probably should have had a goal early on, sending a header over the bar.

It seemed inevitable that France would make the final. They could do it all – be hard to score against and, like a flick of a switch, turn into the most dangerous attacking team. They met Belgium in the semi-final. They were a formidable opponent, probably tougher than Argentina.

Belgium thought it was their best chance to win a World Cup. They had star players such as Eden Hazard, Romelu Lukaku, Vincent Kompany and Kevin De Bruyne. Most teams would be nervous about facing such talent. Not Kylian. On the plane journey to St Petersburg for the biggest game of his life, Kylian fell asleep!

He was right not to worry. France won 1–0 in a game which did not live up to the hype. Again, Kylian missed an early chance but he didn't care – he was going to the World Cup Final! "What a dream!" he wrote on his Instagram page. Croatia and their brilliant playmaker Luka Modrić stood between France and glory.

# CHAMPION
# OF THE WORLD

Waiting in the tunnel before the final Kylian nodded and smiled at Ousmane Dembélé again. But he had also been thinking back to that fateful Wednesday in the Coupe 93 final in the stadium in Gagny when, aged eleven, he was scared of failure, earning a telling off from his mum. He had come a long way. *This is no time to be nervous*, he thought. *Enjoy it!*

The best way for Kylian to relax and enjoy the biggest match in the world was to get on the ball and hurt Croatia. He got straight on with it, getting into the penalty area down the right side and almost finding a teammate with a cross. He then sprinted with the ball towards the goal, only to be stopped by a tackle. Almost!

Antoine Griezmann was having more luck and was causing Croatia all sorts of problems. At half-time, France were 2–1 up thanks to a clever free kick from their playmaker Luka Modrić that caused an own goal and a penalty.

In the second half Kylian was used as a counter-attacking threat. And one that paid off in the fifty-ninth minute. His cross was worked to Paul Pogba on the edge of the area and he smashed it home. 3–1 to France!

### Final Flourish

Kylian would not be denied his goal. And it was the best of the lot. He sent a rasping shot past the goalkeeper from more than twenty yards. He was the first teenager to score in a World Cup final in sixty years – the last being Brazil legend Pelé. "Welcome to the club," Pelé later tweeted to Mbappé.

Kylian still felt he was dreaming as France lifted the trophy with gold confetti floating in the air. He kissed the trophy and said he never wanted to let it go.

*Championes! Championes! Championes!* The French players sang and danced.

Naturally, Kylian was awarded the best young player of the tournament. Emmanuel Macron, the French president, presented him with the award.

"You're a French national hero now," he said. "Thank you."

"My pleasure, sir."

When Kylian and his teammates returned to France they had an open-top bus parade of Paris. Thousands lined the streets to celebrate with them.

But Kylian was not fussed. He wanted to be at home. "Isn't this a bit much?" he said. He wanted to relax and rest, focusing on returning to playing and more trophies. It was just like when he had won the European Under-19 tournament and Monaco's league title.

"Top players aren't happy with what they have already done, so the aim is to win more and more," he said.

# EPILOGUE

# BUSINESS AS USUAL

Having won the World Cup at just nineteen and been compared to Pelé, some people thought that Kylian wouldn't have the hunger or desire to keep on scoring goals, making them and winning titles. What was there left to achieve, to work hard for? They didn't know him very well.

Ever since he was a young boy at Bondy he was angered by people saying that his age was a barrier to achieving what he wanted. He felt that in those early days in Monaco too, when the coaches said he was too immature. Kylian's philosophy was "if you're good enough, you're old enough".

Not only did Kylian play like someone who was much older, he spoke with wisdom beyond his years too.

"We can be the best and the world champions, as we are now," he said after the World Cup. "And in four years, you are forgotten, because there is someone else who has arrived and done better than you."

Kylian wanted to build a legacy. So when he returned to Ligue 1 action with Paris Saint-Germain there was no sign that Kylian had lost any of his speed, skill or determination. And so the honours followed again.

In the 2018–19 season the Trophée des Champions was won in August, followed by a stroll to Ligue 1 title by a massive sixteen points. Kylian, now wearing the number 7 shirt as a sign of his rise to senior player status, was the top scorer in the league with thirty-three goals.

All over the world he was seen as an icon. He designed a clothing range with Nike. Madame Tussauds made a waxwork of him. And other players would copy him. The boy who borrowed Cristiano Ronaldo's celebrations had players impersonating him. Liverpool's Trent Alexander-Arnold and

Arsenal's Gabriel Martinelli both copied his goal celebration.

The following season, the coronavirus pandemic hit. The Ligue 1 season was abandoned. PSG were awarded another title, having been twelve points clear of Marseille at the time. Kylian was named top scorer, despite being level on eighteen with Monaco's Wissam Ben Yedder. Kylian edged out Wissam because he had scored more goals from open play. Kylian also had a better goals-per-game ratio, scoring his eighteen goals in twenty games, compared with Wissam's twenty-six.

Still, PSG had failed in 2018–19 to win the Champions League. It was their ultimate goal. They knew there was no point thrashing teams week in and week out in France if they couldn't go to the next level. Kylian was frustrated at their failure and after receiving the player of the season trophy he stunned everyone by saying in his speech: "I've arrived at a first or second turning point of my career. I feel now is the time to have more responsibility. I hope this will be at PSG … or maybe I will go somewhere else."

With no football to play and normal life grinding to a halt because of the virus, Kylian concentrated on charity work. At the start of 2020 Kylian had launched his own charity called Inspired by Kylian Mbappé (IBKM). It supported ninety-eight children from all over Paris to help them achieve their dreams, whatever they were.

"When you are children you have a lot of dreams," he said. "A lot of children have potential but don't have the money to do it. I'm here to help. I will be there for them."

Kylian felt it was really important to use his fame to give something back. He knew he was lucky and that so many were less fortunate than him. This was particularly true as the virus swept through Europe. He donated money to help homeless people get shelter and food with Paris in lockdown.

This wasn't a new idea to Kylian. After the World Cup he donated his entire earnings from the competition – more than £400,000 – to a charity which helps disabled children learn sports.

Kylian was building a legacy off the pitch. But there was still plenty left to do on it. When football returned Kylian and PSG won the French Cup. But Kylian's dream of a Champions League win was dashed again after a special eight-team knockout tournament was organized in Lisbon, Portugal, in

August with no fans allowed. PSG had made it to their first ever final after beating Italian team Atalanta in the quarter-finals and German side RB Leipzig in the semi-finals. But they could not find a way past Bayern Munich, losing 1–0. Kylian had missed a good chance to put PSG in the lead just before Kingsley Coman scored the winner.

Unlike the Champions League, the European Championships in 2020 had been postponed until the following year, meaning Kylian and France would have to wait to see if they could hold both world and European titles at the same time. And the rumours about a move to Real Madrid would not go away.

The boy wonder had never made it a secret that he wanted to win titles in as many of the big leagues as possible. He wanted to win everything, everywhere. Again and again. And few would doubt he could do it.

# Timeline

| | |
|---|---|
| **12 July 1998** | France win their first World Cup, beating Brazil 3–0 in the final. |
| **20 December 1998** | Kylian is born in Bondy, near Paris, France. |
| **2004** | Kylian starts to play for AS Bondy, aged six. |
| **2010** | Aged eleven, travels to London to have a trial with Chelsea, playing a match against Charlton Athletic. |
| **2011** | Joins the famous Clairefontaine academy but continues to play for AS Bondy. |
| **2012** | Has a week's trial at Real Madrid. |

| | |
|---|---|
| **2012** | Joins AS Monaco at age fourteen on a three-year youth contract, rejecting a host of top clubs including Real Madrid, Chelsea, Manchester City, Liverpool, Bayern Munich. |
| **2015** | Scores his first goal for Monaco B, the club's reserve team. Scores four goals in fourteen matches for the reserves. |
| **2 December 2015** | Makes his first-team debut against SM Caen and becomes the youngest ever Monaco player at sixteen years and 347 days, breaking record set by the legendary Thierry Henry twenty-one years before. |
| **20 February 2016** | Scores his first Monaco goal in a 3–1 win over Troyes. At the age of seventeen years and sixty-two days he is the club's youngest ever goalscorer, taking the record from Thierry Henry. |

| | |
|---|---|
| **6 March 2016** | Signs first professional contract, a three-year deal with Monaco. |
| **15 July 2016** | Playing for France in the Under-19 European Championship, Kylian scores his team's second goal against Croatia. He then scores a double against the Netherlands to qualify for the knockouts. |
| **21 July 2016** | Almost single-handedly he fires France into the final with two more goals. |
| **24 July 2016** | France win the Under-19 European Championship by beating Italy in the final. |
| **14 December 2016** | Scores his first hat-trick in a 7–0 hammering of Stade Rennais in the French League Cup. |
| **11 February 2017** | Scores his first league hat-trick in a 5–0 win over Metz. At eighteen years and two months he is the youngest ever to score three goals in a Ligue 1 game. |

| 21 February 2017 | Scores his first goal in a European competition against Manchester City and in doing so becomes the second youngest French goalscorer in Champions League. |
| --- | --- |
| 5 March 2017 | Scores twice in a 4–0 home Monaco win against FC Nantes. This takes Kylian's Ligue 1 career goal tally to ten, the youngest in thirty years to have achieved it. He has played just 822 minutes of football. |
| 15 March 2017 | Monaco beat Manchester 3–1 in the second leg of the Champions League to make it to the quarter-finals. Kylian scores the first goal. It is his eleventh goal in his past eleven matches. |
| March 2017 | Kylian is picked in the France national team squad for matches against Luxembourg and Spain. |

**25 March**

Kylian makes his debut for France against Luxembourg as a substitute. At eighteen years, three months and five days he is the second-youngest ever to play for his country.

**11 April 2017**

In the quarter-final, Kylian scores a double away to Borussia Dortmund in the first leg to win 3–2. He scores again in the home leg as Monaco win 3–1. Unfortunately Monaco are eliminated by Juventus in the semi-finals, but Kylian scored their only goal.

| | |
|---|---|
| **May 2017** | Monaco win the Ligue 1 title. Kylian ends the 2016–17 season with twenty-six goals from forty-four matches in all competitions. He scores fifteen league goals, making him the joint fifth-highest scorer. He is seventh on the list of most assists with eight. He wins the Ligue 1 Young Player of the Year award. |
| **31 August 2017** | Kylian gets his first senior international goal in a 3–1 victory over the Netherlands in a World Cup qualifier. |
| | On the same day Paris Saint-Germain announce that they have signed Kylian on loan from Monaco. Kylian will become the second-most expensive player ever. |

| | |
|---|---|
| **8 September 2017** | Kylian scores on his debut for PSG away to Metz. Four days later he scores again – his first European goal for his new team in the Champions League against Scottish giants Celtic. |
| **6 December 2017** | Another record for Kylian. A goal against Bayern Munich in the Champions League gives him ten for the most famous tournament – the youngest player to reach such a mark, at eighteen years and eleven months. |
| **8 May 2018** | PSG win the Coupe de France, the most prestigious cup competition in the country, and Kylian scores to see off Les Herbiers VF. |
| **17 May 2018** | Kylian is going to the World Cup! He is selected in the squad for the tournament in Russia. |

| | |
|---|---|
| **21 June 2018** | He makes history in the 1–0 win over Peru in the World Cup. At nineteen he is France's youngest ever goalscorer in the tournament. |
| **30 June 2018** | Kylian wins the man of the match award in the 4–3 win over Argentina in the first knockout match at the World Cup. He wins a penalty for Antoine Griezmann and scores two. |
| **July 2018** | Kylian is given the famous number 7 shirt by PSG. |
| **8 October 2018** | In just thirteen minutes Kylian scores four goals in a 5–0 home victory over Lyon. He also becomes the youngest player (nineteen years and nine months) to score four goals in one game in Ligue 1 for forty-five years. |
| **19 January 2019** | Kylian scores a hat-trick in a 9–0 win over Guingamp. |

| | |
|---|---|
| **2 March 2019** | Against Caen, Kylian scores twice, the second his fiftieth goal for PSG. |
| **May 2019** | PSG win the Ligue 1 title. Kylian is named player of the year. He is also the league's top goalscorer with thirty-three. |
| **11 June 2019** | Kylian scores his 100th career goal – netting for France against Andorra in a qualifying match for the 2020 European Championship. |
| **3 August 2019** | Kylian scores in a 2–1 win over Rennes as PSG win the first title of the new French season: the Trophée des Champions. |

| | |
|---|---|
| **22 October 2019** | From the substitutes' bench Kylian scores a hat-trick against Club Brugge, a team from Belgium, in the Champions League. It means at the age of twenty years and 306 days he is the youngest to ever score fifteen goals in the competition. |
| **1 May 2020** | PSG are named Ligue 1 winners after the coronavirus pandemic forces the abandonment of the season. Kylian is the league's top goalscorer. |
| **July 2020** | PSG and Kylian win the French Cup. |

# Records and Honours

## Kylian's Team Honours

*France*
2018      World Cup
2016      Under-19 European Championship

*Paris Saint-Germain*
2019–20  Ligue 1, Coupe de la Ligue, Coupe de France
2019      Trophée des Champions
2018–19  Ligue 1
2017–18  Ligue 1, Coupe de la Ligue, Coupe de France

*Monaco*
2016–17  Ligue 1

## Kylian's Individual Honours

Kylian's first award was being named in the team of the tournament in the European Under-19 championship.

He won the Ligue 1 Player of the Year award for the first time for the 2018–19 season.

Three times he has been named the Ligue 1 Young Player of the Year: in 2017, 2018 and 2019. In each of those years he was also named in the Ligue 1 Team of the Year.

He has won five Ligue 1 Player of the Month awards: April 2017, March 2018, February 2019 and February 2021.

After Monaco's 2016–17 season, Kylian was honoured to be named in the Champions League Squad of the Season alongside his idol Cristiano Ronaldo and Lionel Messi. The judges said: "The outstanding young player in an outstanding team of young players. Excellent strike play throughout."

Twice (in 2018 and 2019) Kylian has been named in the FIFPro World XI. FIFPro is the worldwide organisation to help and support footballers.

Kylian has never won the Ballon d'Or (Golden

Ball), the most coveted individual award which recognises the best player in the world. But it is a big ambition. He came seventh in 2017 and fourth in 2018. It is an award dominated by Cristiano Ronaldo and Lionel Messi. Between them they have won eleven of the last twelve.

After his sensational performance in France's World Cup triumph, Kylian was named in the Team of the Tournament and won the Best Young Player award.

Twice he has won the French Player of the Year award, in 2018 and 2019.

He was named in UEFA's Team of the Year in 2018.

In the 2018–19 Ligue 1 season Kylian was top goalscorer with thirty-three goals at a rate of 1.1 per game. In 2019–20 he was top again! This time with eighteen goals at a rate of 0.9 per game.

# Kylian's Clubs

## Monaco

**Club name:** *AS Monaco*
**Nickname:** The Monégasques, the Red and Whites
**Short name:** Monaco
**Founded:** 1924
**Current manager:** Niko Kovač
**Current league:** Ligue 1
**Crest:** A gold shield with red and white stripes, topped with a crown

## Paris Saint-Germain

**Club name:** *Paris Saint-Germain*
**Nickname:** The Parisians, The Red and Blues
**Short name:** PSG
**Founded:** 1970
**Current manager:** Mauricio Pochettino
**Current league:** Ligue 1
**Crest:** A blue circle with a red Eiffel Tower in the centre

## Appearances and Goals

**Monaco**

2015–2018
41 appearances, 16 goals

**Paris Saint-Germain**

2017–present
123 appearances, 106 goals

**France**

2017–present
42 appearances, 16 goals

## Kylian's Favourite Goals

### First professional goal

**When:** 20 February 2016
**Playing:** Troyes
**How it happened:** With Troyes trailing 2–1 and pushing high up the pitch for an equaliser, they are caught out by a breakaway. The ball is played across the left of the area to Kylian, whose speed takes him away from the defender and he shoots first time, lifting the ball over the goalkeeper into the centre of the goal.

## First European goal

When: 21 February 2017
Playing: Manchester City
How it happened: Playing for Monaco, Kylian is played in behind the Manchester City defence. Defender Nicolás Otamendi thinks he has the eighteen-year-old covered, but he is taken by surprise by the youngster's amazing speed and he is left trailing. Kylian zeroes in on goal and shoots high over the goalkeeper to give Monaco a 2–1 lead.

## First goal for France

When: 31 August 2017
Playing: Netherlands
How it happened: This is one of the easiest goals of his career but one of the most important, as it shows he can be a top international player. The Netherlands' defence is all over the place as a cross finds its way to the back post and Kylian makes no mistake, slamming the ball home to give France the lead.

## First goal for Paris Saint-Germain

**When:** 8 September 2017
**Playing:** Metz
**How it happened:** On his PSG debut Kylian tries to play an outrageous chip pass to put Neymar in on goal. But the defender cut it out. The ball drops back to Kylian right on the edge of the area and without breaking his stride he smashes a low shot into the goal. All his PSG teammates come to celebrate with him as they know the first goal for a new club is so special.

## First goal in the World Cup final

**When:** 15 July 2018
**Playing:** Croatia
**How it happened:** After great tricky play by Lucas Hernandez on the left wing, Kylian is passed the ball twenty-five yards out from goal. He quickly moves into a shooting position and, with his right foot, cuts across the ball with a wicked shot to wrong-foot the goalkeeper to make history. He runs away and his mobbed by his teammates before he can even finish his trademark celebration.

## Did You Know?

Kylian is very active on social media. He has 5.9 million followers on Twitter and more than 50 million followers on Instagram! He uses his accounts to remind his followers of the importance of family, to highlight good causes, such as the Black Lives Matter campaign, or during the coronavirus to remind fans to wear face masks.

Kylian is not just famous for his footballing brilliance. He is famous for being wise beyond his years. Benjamin Mendy, his France teammate and former Monaco teammate, has nicknamed him 'my little Obama' after the American President Barack Obama. Why? Because he listens carefully to questions and gives thoughtful answers.

Between the ages of six and eleven Kylian attended a centre for performing arts in Paris, where he learned to sing, read music and play the flute.

Kylian can speak Spanish. He started taking lessons in 2019 and is known to speak fluently in the language with Neymar in the PSG dressing room. Neymar learned when he was at Barcelona.